Her HEART His PROMISES

A 31-Day Women's Prayer Guide

LATONNE ADESANYA

31 Day Prayer and Interactive Journal for Women

Copyright © 2025 by Latonne Adesanya
All rights reserved. No part of this book may be reproduced, distributed, or transmitted in any form or by any means, including photocopying, recording, or other electronic or mechanical methods, without the prior written consent of the copyright owner, except in case of brief quotation embodied in critical articles, reviews, and certain other noncommercial uses permitted by copyright law.

>> INTRODUCTION

Welcome to your 31-day journey of prayer, reflection, and growth. This guide is designed to help you deepen your relationship with God, explore His promises, and discover how His Word can empower and transform your life. Each day includes a scripture, a devotional reflection, a prayer, and space for you to write your thoughts and prayers. Let this be a sacred time for you to draw closer to God and to embrace your identity as His beloved daughter.

Day 1 ≫ Psalm 46:5

VERSE "God is within her; she will not fall; God will help her at break of day."

REFLECTION God's presence in your life means that no obstacle can outweigh His power. Trust that He is your strength and ever-present help. Even in times of uncertainty, He upholds you.

PRAYER Lord, thank You for being my refuge and strength. Help me to trust in Your power and not fear the challenges ahead. Let me walk boldly, knowing You are within me.

YOUR THOUGHTS:

≫ What obstacles do you need to trust God with today?

≫ How does knowing God is with you change your perspective?

Day 2 » Luke 1:45

VERSE "Blessed is she who has believed that the Lord would fulfill his promises to her!"

REFLECTION Believing in God's promises brings blessings and peace. What promises are you holding onto? Faith opens the door for His blessings to unfold in your life.

PRAYER Father, I believe in Your promises. Strengthen my faith when I doubt and remind me that Your Word never fails. I trust in Your plans for my life.

YOUR THOUGHTS:

» What promises from God are you waiting to see fulfilled?
_____
_____

» How can you strengthen your belief in His faithfulness?
_____
_____

Day 3 » Proverbs 31:25

VERSE "She is clothed with strength and dignity; she can laugh at the days to come."

REFLECTION Strength and dignity are your spiritual attire. Laughing at the future comes from knowing that God holds your tomorrows. Release fear and embrace joy.

PRAYER Lord, thank You for clothing me with strength and dignity. Help me to trust You with my future and to live with a joyful heart, free from worry.

YOUR THOUGHTS:

» What areas of your life need God's strength today?

» How can you laugh at the future with faith?

Day 4 >> Proverbs 11:6

VERSE "The righteousness of the upright delivers them, but the unfaithful are trapped by evil desires."

REFLECTION Living righteously brings freedom and deliverance. God's ways protect you from harmful paths. Seek His guidance in every decision.

PRAYER Lord, lead me in Your righteousness. Deliver me from anything that would trap me, and help me walk in Your truth.

YOUR THOUGHTS:

>> What decisions do you need to bring before God?

>> How does righteousness set you free?

Day 5 » Proverbs 14:1

VERSE "The wise woman builds her house, but with her own hands the foolish one tears hers down."

REFLECTION Your words and actions have the power to build or destroy. Choose wisdom in nurturing your relationships and home.

PRAYER Father, grant me the wisdom to build my home with love, peace, and understanding. Guard my words and actions, that they may reflect Your heart.

YOUR THOUGHTS:

» How are you building or tearing down your home?

» What steps can you take to be a wise woman?

Day 6 » Proverbs 31:26-27

VERSE "She speaks with wisdom, and faithful instruction is on her tongue. She watches over the affairs of her household and does not eat the bread of idleness."

REFLECTION Your words and actions can inspire and guide those around you. Speak with wisdom and remain diligent in your responsibilities.

PRAYER Lord, help me to speak words of wisdom and encouragement. Give me the strength to faithfully manage all that You have entrusted to me.

YOUR THOUGHTS:

» How can you use your words to uplift others?

» What areas of your life need more diligence?

Day 7 » Colossians 4:5-6

VERSE "Be wise in the way you act toward outsiders; make the most of every opportunity. Let your conversation be always full of grace, seasoned with salt, so that you may know how to answer everyone."

REFLECTION Your actions and words can leave a lasting impact on others. Approach every interaction with wisdom and grace, letting God's love shine through you. Each moment is an opportunity to reflect His character.

PRAYER Lord, help me to act wisely and speak graciously to everyone I meet. May my words bring life and hope, and may my actions draw others closer to You.

YOUR THOUGHTS:

» How can you make the most of the opportunities God gives you?

» In what ways can your words be seasoned with grace?

Day 8 » Proverbs 31:16

VERSE "She considers a field and buys it; out of her earnings she plants a vineyard."

REFLECTION God calls you to be thoughtful and resourceful in your decisions. Like the Proverbs 31 woman, use wisdom and initiative to create blessings for your household and community.

PRAYER Lord, guide me in making wise decisions that honor You. Help me to be resourceful and proactive, using the gifts You've given me to bless others.

YOUR THOUGHTS:

» How can you be resourceful with what God has entrusted to you?

» What areas of your life require thoughtful planning?

Day 9 » Luke 1:45

VERSE "Blessed is she who has believed that the Lord would fulfill his promises to her!"

REFLECTION Faith unlocks the blessings of God's promises. Your belief in His Word creates room for miracles in your life. Trust that His plans for you are good.

PRAYER Lord, I hold onto Your promises with confidence. Strengthen my faith and guide me to live as a testimony of Your faithfulness.

YOUR THOUGHTS:

» What promises of God encourage you most?

» How can you deepen your trust in Him?

Day 10 » Psalm 34:4

VERSE "I sought the Lord, and he answered me; he delivered me from all my fears."

REFLECTION God is faithful to answer when you call. Seek Him with all your heart, and let Him deliver you from fear. In His presence, you find peace and courage.

PRAYER Father, thank You for hearing me when I seek You. Deliver me from my fears and fill me with Your peace. Help me to trust in You completely.

YOUR THOUGHTS:

» What fears do you need to bring before God today?

» How has God delivered you in the past?

Day 11 ≫ Psalm 139:14

VERSE "I praise you because I am fearfully and wonderfully made; your works are wonderful, I know that full well."

REFLECTION You are God's masterpiece, created with purpose and beauty. Embrace your uniqueness and know that you are loved deeply by Him.

PRAYER Lord, thank You for creating me wonderfully and uniquely. Help me to see myself through Your eyes and to live confidently in my identity in You.

YOUR THOUGHTS:

≫ What do you love about the way God made you?
_____
_____

≫ How can you embrace your uniqueness today?
_____
_____

Day 12 >> Proverbs 31:28

VERSE *"Her children arise and call her blessed; her husband also, and he praises her."*

REFLECTION Your influence and love leave a lasting impact on those around you. Live a life that inspires others to see the goodness of God in you.

PRAYER Father, may my life reflect Your love and faithfulness. Help me to nurture and inspire those in my care to honor You.

YOUR THOUGHTS:

>> How can you live a life that inspires others to praise God?

>> Who in your life do you need to encourage or bless today?

Day 13 » Proverbs 3:15

VERSE "She is more precious than rubies; nothing you desire can compare with her."

REFLECTION God values you more than the finest treasures. Walk confidently, knowing that you are cherished beyond measure.

PRAYER Lord, thank You for seeing me as precious and valuable. Help me to live in a way that honors the worth You've placed on my life.

YOUR THOUGHTS:

» How does knowing you are precious to God impact your self-worth?

» What steps can you take to honor God's value in your life?

Day 14 » 1 Peter 3:3-4

VERSE "Your beauty should not come from outward adornment, such as elaborate hairstyles and the wearing of gold jewelry or fine clothes. Rather, it should be that of your inner self, the unfading beauty of a gentle and quiet spirit, which is of great worth in God's sight."

REFLECTION True beauty shines from within. Let your gentle spirit and inner strength reflect God's love and grace to the world around you.

PRAYER Lord, help me to focus on the beauty of my heart and spirit. Let my inner self radiate Your love and reflect Your glory.

YOUR THOUGHTS:

» How can you cultivate inner beauty?

» What does true beauty mean to you?

Day 15 » Proverbs 31:20-21

VERSE "She opens her arms to the poor and extends her hands to the needy. When it snows, she has no fear for her household; for all of them are clothed in scarlet."

REFLECTION A heart of generosity and preparation reflects God's provision and care. Be a blessing to others while trusting God to meet your needs.

PRAYER Father, help me to extend my hands to those in need and to prepare for my family with wisdom and faith. Let my life reflect Your kindness and care.

YOUR THOUGHTS:

» How can you be more generous today?
_____
_____

» In what ways can you prepare for the needs of those you love
_____
_____

Day 16 » Proverbs 31:30-31

VERSE "Charm is deceptive, and beauty is fleeting; but a woman who fears the Lord is to be praised. Honor her for all that her hands have done, and let her works bring her praise at the city gate."

REFLECTION A life that honors God brings lasting impact and praise. Let your actions reflect your reverence for Him, knowing that His approval is the greatest reward.

PRAYER Lord, I desire to live a life that honors You above all else. Help me to focus on what truly matters and to serve You with all my heart.

YOUR THOUGHTS:

» What does it mean to you to fear the Lord?

» How can your works reflect God's glory today?

Day 17 » Genesis 2:18-24

VERSE "The Lord God said, 'It is not good for the man to be alone. I will make a helper suitable for him.'"

REFLECTION Relationships are a gift from God, designed for companionship and support. Whether married or single, cherish the connections God places in your life.

PRAYER Father, thank You for the gift of relationships. Help me to nurture and value the people You've brought into my life, and to reflect Your love in all my interactions.

YOUR THOUGHTS:

» How can you honor the relationships in your life?

» What does being a "helper" mean in your context?

Day 18 >> Proverbs 11:22

> **VERSE** "Like a gold ring in a pig's snout is a beautiful woman who shows no discretion."

REFLECTION True beauty is found in wisdom and discretion. Let your actions and words reflect integrity and thoughtfulness, honoring God in all you do.

PRAYER Lord, grant me the wisdom to live with discretion and grace. Let my actions bring honor to You and reflect the beauty of Your Spirit in me.

YOUR THOUGHTS:

>> How can you demonstrate discretion in your daily life?

>> What qualities do you want others to see in you?

Day 19 >> Proverbs 31:10

VERSE

"A wife of noble character who can find? She is worth far more than rubies."

REFLECTION

A woman of noble character reflects integrity, kindness, and a heart aligned with God. Your worth is not determined by worldly standards but by the value God places on your life.

PRAYER

Lord, help me cultivate a heart of noble character. May my actions, thoughts, and words reflect Your righteousness and love. Teach me to walk in a way that honors You.

YOUR THOUGHTS:

>> What qualities define a woman of noble character in your life?

>> How can you embrace your worth in God today?

Day 20 » Titus 2:4-5

VERSE "Then they can urge the younger women to love their husbands and children, to be self-controlled and pure, to be busy at home, to be kind, and to be subject to their husbands, so that no one will malign the word of God."

REFLECTION As women, we are called to model love, self-control, and kindness. Your influence can shape the next generation and bring honor to God's Word.

PRAYER Father, guide me to be an example of love and purity. Help me live in a way that encourages others to know You and reflects Your Word in my daily life.

YOUR THOUGHTS:

» How can you mentor or encourage younger women in your community?

» What areas of your life need more self-control or kindness?

Day 21 >> Proverbs 31:25

VERSE "She is clothed with strength and dignity; she can laugh at the days to come."

REFLECTION Strength and dignity are your spiritual armor. Trusting God with your future allows you to laugh without fear of what lies ahead.

PRAYER Lord, thank You for clothing me with strength and dignity. Help me to face the future with joy, knowing that You hold my tomorrows in Your hands.

YOUR THOUGHTS:

>> What worries about the future can you release to God today?
_____
_____

>> How can you live in strength and dignity in your daily life?
_____
_____

Day 22 >> Proverbs 31:27

VERSE *"She watches over the affairs of her household and does not eat the bread of idleness."*

REFLECTION God calls you to be diligent in caring for your responsibilities. Your work, whether at home or elsewhere, is meaningful and honors Him when done with love and purpose.

PRAYER Father, help me to be diligent and faithful in my responsibilities. Teach me to manage my time wisely and to serve You in all I do.

YOUR THOUGHTS:

>> In what areas of your life do you need more diligence?
_____
_____

>> How can you bring purpose to your daily tasks?
_____
_____

Day 23 >> Matthew 5:8

VERSE "Blessed are the pure in heart, for they will see God."

REFLECTION Purity of heart brings clarity in seeing God's presence and purpose in your life. Seek to align your heart with His will and allow His peace to fill you.

PRAYER Lord, create in me a pure heart. Help me to see You in every aspect of my life and to live in a way that reflects Your love and holiness.

YOUR THOUGHTS:

>> How can you strive for a pure heart today?

>> Where have you seen God working in your life recently?

Day 23 » Isaiah 8:18

VERSE "Here am I, and the children the Lord has given me. We are signs and symbols in Israel from the Lord Almighty, who dwells on Mount Zion."

REFLECTION You and your family are created with a divine purpose, meant to reflect God's presence and power to the world. As His chosen ones, your life is a testimony of His love and faithfulness. Embrace the role God has given you to shine His light in your home and beyond.

PRAYER Father, thank You for placing a purpose on my life and my family. Help us to live as signs of Your goodness and faithfulness. Let our lives bring glory to You and draw others closer to Your heart.

YOUR THOUGHTS:

» How can you live as a sign of God's love and faithfulness today?

» What role does your family play in reflecting God's light to others?

Day 25 » 1 Peter 4:8

VERSE "Above all, love each other deeply, because love covers over a multitude of sins."

REFLECTION Deep love rooted in Christ has the power to heal and unite. Extend grace and forgiveness, knowing that love reflects God's heart.

PRAYER Lord, teach me to love deeply and selflessly. Help me to extend grace and forgiveness, and to reflect Your love in all my relationships.

YOUR THOUGHTS:

» Who in your life needs to experience God's love through you?

» How can you practice forgiveness and grace today?

Day 26 » Psalm 34:8

VERSE *"Taste and see that the Lord is good; blessed is the one who takes refuge in him."*

REFLECTION God invites you to experience His goodness firsthand. Trust Him in every circumstance and find refuge in His unchanging love. When you seek Him, you will discover the joy and peace that only He can provide.

PRAYER Lord, thank You for Your goodness and faithfulness. Help me to trust You more each day and to take refuge in Your presence. Open my eyes to see Your blessings in my life.

YOUR THOUGHTS:

» How have you experienced God's goodness recently?

» What areas of your life need more trust and reliance on Him?

Day 27 » Proverbs 18:22

VERSE "He who finds a wife finds what is good and receives favor from the Lord."

REFLECTION Marriage is a gift from God, a reflection of His love and favor. Whether you are single, married, or widowed, embrace your role as a woman of God who brings joy and blessing to others.

PRAYER Father, thank You for the gift of relationships. Help me to be a source of love, encouragement, and blessing to those around me.

YOUR THOUGHTS:

» How can you reflect God's favor in your relationships?

» What qualities do you value most in relationships?

Day 28 » Zechariah 8:12

VERSE "The seed will grow well, the vine will yield its fruit, the ground will produce its crops, and the heavens will drop their dew. I will give all these things as an inheritance to the remnant of this people."

REFLECTION God's promises of provision and abundance are for those who remain faithful. Just as seeds take time to grow, trust that God is working in your life, cultivating blessings that will bear fruit in due season. Stay steadfast, knowing that His plans for you are fruitful and filled with hope.

PRAYER Lord, thank You for being the source of all provision and blessing. Help me to remain faithful as I trust in Your timing and care. May my life bear fruit that reflects Your goodness and glory.

YOUR THOUGHTS:

» What seeds of faith or effort are you planting in your life?

» How can you trust God's promises of provision and abundance today?

Day 29 » Joshua 1:9

VERSE "Have I not commanded you? Be strong and courageous. Do not be afraid; do not be discouraged, for the Lord your God will be with you wherever you go."

REFLECTION God's command to be strong and courageous comes with a promise—He is always with you. Step boldly into His plans, trusting in His guidance.

PRAYER Lord, fill me with Your strength and courage. Help me to overcome fear and discouragement, knowing that You are with me always.

YOUR THOUGHTS:

» What fears can you surrender to God today?
_____
_____

» How can you walk in courage and faith this week?
_____
_____

Day 30 >> Proverbs 31:26

VERSE "She speaks with wisdom, and faithful instruction is on her tongue."

REFLECTION Your words have the power to uplift, encourage, and guide. Let wisdom and faithfulness shape your conversations, pointing others to God's truth.

PRAYER Lord, guide my words to reflect Your wisdom and love. Help me to speak in ways that build others up and bring glory to Your name.

YOUR THOUGHTS:

>> How can you use your words to encourage someone today?

>> What wisdom has God been teaching you recently?

Day 31 » Psalm 127:3

VERSE "Children are a heritage from the Lord, offspring a reward from him."

REFLECTION Whether you have children of your own or nurture others in your life, see them as God's precious gifts. Invest in their lives with love, care, and guidance.

PRAYER Father, thank You for the children and people You've placed in my life. Help me to nurture them with love and wisdom, reflecting Your heart in all I do.

YOUR THOUGHTS:

» Who has God entrusted you to nurture or guide?

» How can you celebrate and cherish the people in your life today?

CLOSING PRAYERS

Heavenly Father,

Thank You for walking with us through this 31-day journey of prayer and reflection. You are a faithful and loving God, and we are in awe of Your goodness. We are grateful for the truths You have revealed through Your Word, the strength You have given us, and the transformation You have begun in our hearts.

Lord, as we close this chapter, we ask for Your continued guidance in our daily lives. Help us to carry the lessons we've learned and the faith we've built into every aspect of our journey. May we always seek You first, trust in Your promises, and walk in the purpose You have designed for us.

Fill our hearts with Your peace, our minds with Your wisdom, and our lives with Your joy. Let our words and actions reflect Your love to the world around us. Strengthen us to be women of faith, courage, and grace, living boldly for Your glory.

We place our families, our dreams, and our futures in Your hands, knowing that You are the author of every good thing. Thank You for loving us unconditionally and for calling us Your daughters.

In Jesus' name, we pray,
Amen.

www.ingramcontent.com/pod-product-compliance
Lightning Source LLC
LaVergne TN
LVHW021953060526
838201LV00049B/1694